Union Publi

Read-About® Geography

Wyoming

By Pam Zollman

Subject Consultant
Richard W. Jones
Editor and Senior Geologist
Wyoming State Geological Survey
Laramie, Wyoming

Reading Consultant
Cecilia Minden-Cupp, PhD
Former Director of the Language and Literacy Program
Harvard Graduate School of Education
Cambridge, Massachusetts

Union Public Library

Children's Press®
A Division of Scholastic Inc.
New York   Toronto   London   Auckland   Sydney
Mexico City   New Delhi   Hong Kong
Danbury, Connecticut

Designer: Herman Adler Design
Photo Researcher: Caroline Anderson
The photo on the cover shows Wyoming's Grand Teton National Park.

Library of Congress Cataloging-in-Publication Data

Zollman, Pam.
  Wyoming / by Pam Zollman.
    p. cm. — (Rookie read-about geography)
  Includes index.
  ISBN-10: 0-516-25389-1 (lib. bdg.)   0-531-16788-7 (pbk.)
  ISBN-13: 978-0-516-25389-3 (lib. bdg.)   978-0-531-16788-5 (pbk.)
  1. Wyoming—Juvenile literature. 2. Wyoming—Geography—Juvenile
literature. I. Title. II. Series.
  F761.3.Z65 2006
  917.8704'33—dc22   2005024798

© 2007 by Scholastic Inc.
All rights reserved. Published simultaneously in Canada.
Printed in Mexico.

CHILDREN'S PRESS, and ROOKIE READ-ABOUT®,
and associated logos are trademarks and/or registered trademarks
of Scholastic Library Publishing. SCHOLASTIC and associated logos
are trademarks and/or registered trademarks of Scholastic Inc.

1 2 3 4 5 6 7 8 9 10 R 16 15 14 13 12 11 10 09 08 07

Why is Wyoming called the Equality State? Wyoming was the first state to let women vote. It was also the first state to let women run in elections.

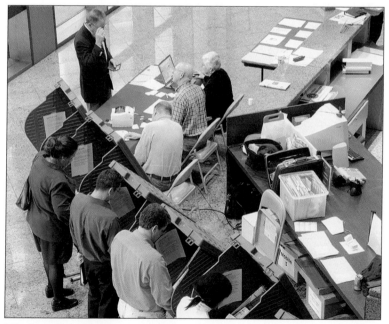

Today, both men and women can vote in U.S. elections.

Wyoming is in the western part of the United States. It touches six other states. Can you find Wyoming on this map?

CANADA

WASHINGTON
OREGON
IDAHO
MONTANA
NORTH DAKOTA
SOUTH DAKOTA
WYOMING
NEBRASKA
NEVADA
UTAH
COLORADO
KANSAS
CALIFORNIA
ARIZONA
NEW MEXICO
OKLAHOMA
TEXAS
MINNESOTA
WISCONSIN
MICHIGAN
IOWA
ILLINOIS
MISSOURI
INDIANA
KENTUCKY
ARKANSAS
TENNESSEE
MISSISSIPPI
ALABAMA
LOUISIANA
NEW HAMPSHIRE
VERMONT
MAINE
NEW YORK
MASSACHUSETTS
RHODE ISLAND
CONNECTICUT
PENNSYLVANIA
NEW JERSEY
OHIO
WEST VIRGINIA
DELAWARE
MARYLAND
VIRGINIA
Washington, D.C.
NORTH CAROLINA
SOUTH CAROLINA
GEORGIA
FLORIDA

North
West   East
South

ALASKA
CANADA
MEXICO
HAWAII

5

Wyoming can be broken into three different sections, or regions.

A herd of bison in the Wyoming Basins Region

The Rocky Mountain Region

They are the Great Plains, Rocky Mountain, and Wyoming Basins regions.

The Great Plains Region has low hills and buttes. A butte is a hill with sloping sides and a flat top.

There are many farms and ranches in the Great Plains Region. Ranchers raise cattle. Farmers grow sugar beets and wheat.

A Wyoming sugar beet farm

Devils Tower

Wyoming's Great Plains Region features mountains called the Black Hills.

Devils Tower is a large block of stone in the Black Hills. It rises more than 1,200 feet (370 meters)! Some people like to climb its rock walls.

Several mountain ranges
come together in the
Rocky Mountain Region.

The Teton Range

The Wind River Range

Some of these are the
Bighorn Mountains,
the Teton Range, and
the Wind River Range.

14

Yellowstone National Park is in Wyoming's Rocky Mountain Region. This park has hot springs and geysers (GYE-zurz).

Geysers are holes in the ground. Hot water and steam shoot up like a fountain from the geysers.

The Wyoming Basins Region is flat and has deep canyons. A canyon is a steep-sided valley.

The Red Desert is in the Wyoming Basins Region. Cacti grow in this dry area.

The Red Desert

This fossil of an ancient fish was found in Wyoming.

Some people find fossils in the Red Desert. Fossils are the hardened remains of plants or animals that lived long ago.

Cheyenne is the capital of Wyoming. It is also the largest city in Wyoming.

Cheyenne has the largest rodeo in the world. This rodeo features cowboys and cowgirls who try to ride bulls and wild horses.

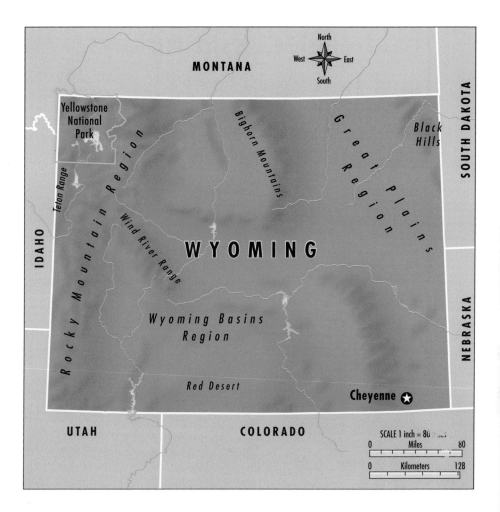

MONTANA

North
West · East
South

Yellowstone
National
Park

Bighorn Mountains

Great Plains Region

Black
Hills

Teton Range

Rocky Mountain Region

Wind River Range

WYOMING

IDAHO

SOUTH DAKOTA

NEBRASKA

Wyoming Basins
Region

Red Desert

Cheyenne ⭐

UTAH

COLORADO

SCALE 1 inch = 80 miles
0   Miles   80

0   Kilometers   128

21

Wyoming is home to
bald eagles, wild turkeys,
and hawks.

A bald eagle

A meadowlark

The state bird is the meadowlark.

Elk, moose, grizzly bears,
and mountain lions live
in Wyoming.

Wyoming's lakes and rivers have many types of fish. Trout, walleye, perch, and catfish all live there.

A perch

A hiker enjoys Wyoming's Beartooth Mountains.

Wyoming has warm summers. People like to camp, hike, and fish.

Winters are long and cold. People enjoy skiing and sledding.

What would you like to
do in Wyoming?

Visitors to Wyoming fish while enjoying a sunset.

Words You Know

bald eagle

Devils Tower

fossils

geysers

grizzly bears

meadowlark

Red Desert

sugar beets

Index

animals, 19, 22–25
bald eagles, 22
Bighorn Mountains, 13
birds, 22–23
Black Hills, 11
bulls, 20
buttes, 8
cacti, 16
camping, 27
canyons, 16
catfish, 25
cattle, 8
Cheyenne, 20
cities, 20
cowboys, 20
cowgirls, 20
deserts, 16, 19
Devils Tower, 11
elections, 3
elk, 24
equality, 3
farms, 8

fish, 25
fishing, 27
fossils, 19
geysers, 15
Great Plains Region, 7, 8, 11
grizzly bears, 24
hawks, 22
hiking, 27
hills, 8
hot springs, 15
lakes, 25
meadowlark (state bird), 23
moose, 24
mountain lions, 24
mountains, 11, 12–13
perch, 25
plants, 16, 19
ranches, 8
Red Desert, 16, 19
rivers, 25
Rocky Mountain Region, 7, 12–13, 15

rodeos, 20
skiing, 27
sledding, 27
state bird, 23
state capital, 20
state nickname, 3
sugar beets, 8
summers, 27
Teton Range, 13
trout, 25
voting, 3
walleye, 25
wheat, 8
wild horses, 20
wild turkeys, 22
Wind River Range, 13
winters, 27
women, 3
Wyoming Basins Region, 7, 16
Yellowstone National Park, 15

About the Author

Pam Zollman is the award-winning author of short stories and books for kids. She is a native Texan who now lives in rural Pennsylvania. She would love to go to Yellowstone National Park someday. Pam dedicates this book to Eileen Robinson, her editor and friend.

Photo Credits

Photographs © 2007: Alamy Images/Chad Ehlers: 29; Corbis Images: 22, 30 top left (W. Perry Conway), 9, 31 bottom right (Royalty-Free); Danita Delimont Stock Photography/ Scott Smith: 13, 17, 18, 30 bottom left, 31 bottom left; Dembinsky Photo Assoc./Alan G. Nelson: 23, 31 top right; National Geographic Image Collection: 6 (Mark Heifner/ Panoramic Images), 26 (Kate Thompson); Nature Picture Library Ltd./Aflo: cover; NHPA/ Lutra: 25; Peter Arnold Inc./Mike Powles: 24, 31 top left; Photo Researchers, NY: 14, 30 bottom right (Bernhard Edmaier), 12 (G. Brad Lewis); PhotoEdit/Bob Daemmrich: 3; Ric Ergenbright: 7, 10, 30 top right.
Maps by Bob Italiano